# JAPANESE

## *Made Nice & Easy!*™

**Staff of Research & Education Association**
**Carl Fuchs, Language Program Director**

**Based on Language Courses developed by the**
**U.S. Government for Foreign Service Personnel**

**Research & Education Association**
61 Ethel Road West
Piscataway, New Jersey 08854

**Dr. M. Fogiel, Director**

# JAPANESE MADE NICE & EASY™

# What This Guide Will Do For You

Whether travelling to a foreign country or to your favorite international restaurant, this *Nice & Easy* guide gives you just enough of the language to get around and be understood. Much of the material in this book was developed for government personnel who are often assigned to a foreign country on a moment's notice and need a quick introduction to the language.

In this handy and compact guide, you will find useful words and phrases, popular expressions, common greetings, and the words for numbers, money, and time. Every word or phrase is accompanied with the correct pronunciation. There is a vocabulary list for finding words quickly.

Generous margins on the pages allow you to make notes and remarks that you may find helpful.

If you expect to travel to Japan, the section on the country's history and relevant up-to-date facts will make your trip more informative and enjoyable. By keeping this guide with you, you'll be well prepared to understand as well as converse in Japanese.

Carl Fuchs
Language Program Director

# Contents

# JAPAN

## Facts & History

### Geography
Area: 377,765 sq. km. (145,856 sq. mi.); slightly smaller than California.
Cities: *Capital*—Tokyo. *Other cities*—Yokohama, Osaka, Nagoya, Sapporo, Kobe, Kyoto, Fukuoka.
Terrain: Rugged, mountainous islands.
Climate: Varies from subtropical to temperate.

### People
Nationality: *Noun and adjective*--Japanese.
Population: 126.2 million.
Population growth rate: 0.23%.
Ethnic groups: Japanese; Korean (0.6%).
Religions: Shinto and Buddhist; Christian (about 1%).
Language: Japanese.

Education: *Literacy*—99%.
Health: *Infant mortality rate*—4/1,000. *Life expectancy*—males 77 yrs., females 83 yrs.
Work force (67 million, 2000): *Services*—23%; *trade, manufacturing, mining, and construction*—56%; *agriculture, forestry, fisheries*—6%; *government*—3%.

## Government
Type: Constitutional monarchy with a parliamentary government.
Constitution: May 3, 1947.
Branches: *Executive*—prime minister (head of government).
*Legislative*—bicameral Diet (House of Representatives and House of Councillors). *Judicial*—civil law system based on the model of Roman law.
Administrative subdivisions: 47 prefectures.
Political parties: Liberal Democratic Party (LDP), Democratic Party of Japan (DPJ), Komeito, Liberal Party, Conservative Party, Japan Communist Party (JCP), Social Democratic Party (SDP).

## People
Japan is one of the most densely populated nations in the world, with some 330 persons per square kilometer (almost 860 persons per sq. mi.). The population growth rate is about 0.23%. Japan's low population growth rate in recent years has raised concerns about the social implications of an aging

population.

The Japanese are a Mongoloid people, closely related to the major groups of East Asia. However, some evidence also exists of a mixture with Malayan and Caucasoid strains. About 750,000 Koreans and much smaller groups of Chinese and Caucasians reside in Japan. Buddhism is important in Japan's religious life and has strongly influenced fine arts, social institutions, and philosophy. Most Japanese consider themselves members of one of the major Buddhist sects.

Shintoism is an indigenous religion founded on myths, legends, and ritual practices of the early Japanese. Neither Buddhism nor Shintoism is an exclusive religion. Most Japanese observe both Buddhist and Shinto rituals: the former for funerals and the latter for births, marriages, and other occasions. Confucianism, primarily an ethical system, profoundly influences Japanese thought as well. About 1.3 million people in Japan are Christians, of whom 60% are Protestant and 40% Roman Catholic.

Japan provides free public schooling for all children through junior high school. Ninety-four percent of students go on to 3-year senior high schools, and competition is stiff for entry into the best universities. Japan enjoys one of the world's highest literacy rates (99%), and nearly 90% of Japanese students complete high school.

# History of Japan

Traditional Japanese legend maintains that Japan was founded in 600 BC by the Emperor Jimmu, a direct descendant of the sun goddess and ancestor of the present ruling imperial family. About AD 405, the Japanese court officially adopted the Chinese writing system. During the sixth century, Buddhism was introduced. These two events revolutionized Japanese culture and marked the beginning of a long period of Chinese cultural influence. From the establishment of the first fixed capital at Nara in 710 until 1867, the emperors of the Yamato dynasty were the nominal rulers, but actual power was usually held by powerful court nobles, regents, or "shoguns" (military governors).

## Contact With the West

The first contact with the West occurred about 1542, when a Portuguese ship, blown off its course to China, landed in Japan. During the next century, traders from Portugal, the Netherlands, England, and Spain arrived, as did Jesuit, Dominican, and Franciscan missionaries. During the early part of the 17th century, Japan's shogunate suspected that the traders and missionaries were actually forerunners of a military conquest by European powers. This caused the shogunate to place foreigners under progressively tighter restrictions. Ultimately, Japan forced all foreigners to leave and barred all relations with the outside world except for severely restricted commercial contacts with Dutch and Chinese merchants at Nagasaki. This isolation lasted for 200 years, until Commodore Matthew Perry of the U.S. Navy forced the opening of Japan to the West with the Convention of Kanagawa in 1854.

Within several years, renewed contact with the West profoundly altered Japanese society. The shogunate was forced to resign, and the emperor was restored to power. The "Meiji restoration" of 1868 initiated many reforms. The feudal system was abolished, and numerous Western institutions were adopted, including a Western legal system and constitutional government along quasi-parliamentary lines.

In 1898, the last of the "unequal treaties" with Western powers was removed, signaling Japan's new status among the nations of the world. In a few decades, by creating modern social, educational, economic, military, and industrial systems, the Emperor Meiji's "controlled revolution" had transformed a feudal and isolated state into a world power.

## Wars With China and Russia

Japanese leaders of the late 19th century regarded the Korean Peninsula as a "dagger pointed at the heart of Japan." It was over Korea that Japan became involved in war with the Chinese Empire in 1894-95 and with Russia in 1904-05. The war with China established Japan's dominant interest in Korea, while giving it the Pescadores Islands and Formosa (now Taiwan). After Japan defeated Russia in 1905, the resulting Treaty of Portsmouth awarded Japan certain rights in Manchuria and in southern Sakhalin, which Russia had received in 1875 in exchange for the Kurile Islands. Both wars gave Japan a free hand in Korea, which it formally annexed in 1910.

## World War I to 1952

World War I permitted Japan, which fought on the side of the victorious Allies, to expand its influence in Asia and its territorial holdings in the Pacific. The postwar era brought Japan unprecedented prosperity. Japan went to the peace conference at Versailles in 1919 as one of the great military and industrial powers of the world and received official recognition as one of the "Big Five" of the new international order. It joined the League of Nations and received a mandate over Pacific islands north of the Equator formerly held by Germany.

During the 1920s, Japan progressed toward a democratic system of government. However, parliamentary government was not rooted deeply enough to withstand the economic and political pressures of the 1930s, during which military leaders became increasingly influential.

Japan invaded Manchuria in 1931 and set up the puppet state of Manchukuo. In 1933, Japan resigned from the League of Nations. The Japanese invasion of China in 1937 followed Japan's signing of the "anti-Comintern pact" with Nazi Germany the previous year and was part of a chain of developments culminating in the Japanese attack on the United States at Pearl Harbor, Hawaii on December 7, 1941.

After almost 4 years of war, resulting in the loss of 3 million Japanese lives and the atomic bombings of Hiroshima and Nagasaki, Japan signed an instrument of surrender on the U.S.S. *Missouri* in Tokyo Harbor on September 2, 1945. As a result of World War II, Japan lost all of its overseas possessions and retained only the home islands. Manchukuo was dissolved, and Manchuria was returned to China; Japan renounced all claims to Formosa; Korea was granted independence; southern Sakhalin and the Kuriles were occupied by the U.S.S.R.; and the United States became the sole administering authority of the Ryukyu, Bonin, and Volcano Islands. The 1972 reversion of

Okinawa completed the United States' return of control of these islands to Japan.

After the war, Japan was placed under international control of the Allies through the Supreme Commander, Gen. Douglas MacArthur. U.S. objectives were to ensure that Japan would become a peaceful nation and to establish democratic self-government supported by the freely expressed will of the people. Political, economic, and social reforms were introduced, such as a freely elected Japanese Diet (legislature). The country's constitution took effect on May 3, 1947. The United States and 45 other Allied nations signed the Treaty of Peace with Japan in September 1951. The U.S. Senate ratified the treaty in March 1952, and under the terms of the treaty, Japan regained full sovereignty on April 28, 1952.

## Recent Political Developments

The post-World War II years saw tremendous economic growth in Japan, with the political system dominated by the Liberal Democratic Party (LDP). That total domination lasted until the Diet Lower House elections on July 18, 1993 in which the LDP, in power since the mid-1950s, failed to win a majority and saw the end of its four-decade rule. A coalition of new parties and existing opposition parties formed a governing majority and elected a new prime minister,

Morihiro Hosokawa, in August 1993. In April 1994, Prime Minister Hosokawa resigned. Prime Minister Tsutomu Hata formed the successor coalition government, Japan's first minority government in almost 40 years. Prime Minister Hata resigned less than 2 months later. Prime Minister Tomiichi Murayama formed the next government in June 1994, a coalition of his Japan Socialist Party (JSP), the LDP, and the small Sakigake Party. Prime Minister Murayama served from June 1994 to January 1996. He was succeeded by Prime Minister Ryutaro Hashimoto, who served from January 1996 to July 1998. Prime Minister Hashimoto headed a loose coalition of three parties until the July 1998 Upper House election, when the two smaller parties cut ties with the LDP. Hashimoto resigned due to a poor electoral showing by the LDP in those Upper House elections.

# Government & Politics

Japan is a constitutional monarchy with a parliamentary government. There is universal adult suffrage with a secret ballot for all elective offices. The executive branch is responsible to the Diet, and the judicial branch is independent. Sovereignty, previously embodied in the emperor, is vested in the Japanese people, and the emperor is defined as the symbol of the state. Japan's Government is a parliamentary democracy, with a House of Representatives and a House of Councillors. Executive power is vested in a cabinet composed of a prime minister and ministers of state, all of whom must be civilians. The prime minister must be a member of the Diet and is designated by his colleagues. The prime minister has the power to appoint and remove ministers, a majority of whom must be Diet members.

Japan's judicial system, drawn from customary law, civil law, and Anglo-American common law, consists of several levels of courts, with the Supreme Court as the final judicial authority. The Japanese constitution includes a bill of rights similar to the U.S. Bill of Rights, and the Supreme Court has the right of judicial review. Japanese courts do not use a jury system, and there are no administrative courts or claims courts.

**Mount Fuji**

Heian Jingu shrine

**Confucian temple**

Geisha

## Hints on Pronunciation

All the words and phrases are written in a spelling which you read like English. When you see the Japanese word for "six" spelled *ro-KOO*, give the *oo* the sound it has in the English words, *too, boot*, etc. Each letter or combination of letters is used for the sound it usually stands for in English and it *always* stands for that sound. Thus, *oo* is always pronounced as it is in *too, boot, tooth, roost*, never as anything else. Say these words and then pronounce the vowel sound by itself. That is the sound you must use every time you see *oo* in the Japanese column. If you should use some other sound—for example, the sound of *oo* in *blood*—you may be misunderstood.

Syllables that are accented, that is, pronounced louder than others, are written in capital letters. Hyphens (-) are used to divide words into syllables in order to make them easier to read. A curved line (‿) connecting two letters means that they are pronounced together without any break; for example, *koo-da-SA‿ee* meaning "please."

Golden temple

### Special Points

*AY*

as in *may*, *say*, *play* but don't drawl it the way we do in English. At times it sounds somewhat like the *e* in *let*. Example: *ko-MAY* meaning "raw rice grains."

*0 or OH*

as in *go*, *so*, *oh*, *note*, *joke* but don't drawl it the way we do in English. At times it sounds somewhat like the *aw* in *law*. Example: *DO-ko* meaning "where."

*0‿0*

is the same as the sound above but much longer. Remember not to confuse this sound with the *oo* pronounced as in *boot*. Example: *a-REENG-a-to‿o* meaning "thank you."

Kabuki theater

# USEFUL WORDS AND PHRASES

## GREETINGS AND GENERAL PHRASES

| *English* | *Japanese* |
|---|---|
| **Good morning** | *o-ha⌣ee-YO⌣o* |
| **Good   day** | *KOHN nee-chee-WA* |

| English | Japanese |
|---------|----------|
| Good evening | *kohn-BAHN-wa* |
| Pardon me | *sheet-SOO-ray⌣ee* |

If you want to ask a person something, you call his attention by saying:

| | |
|---------|----------|
| Pardon me a moment | *CHOHT-to, sheet-SOO-ray⌣ee* |
| Thank you | *a-REENG-a-to⌣o* |

In this word, you heard a sound like the *ng* in *ring*. In many parts of Japan you will hear *a-REE-ga-to⌣o*, with a *g* sound.

| | |
|---------|----------|
| Yes | *HA⌣ee* |
| No | *EE⌣yay* |
| Do you understand? | *wa-ka-ree-MA-SKA?* |
| I don't understand | *wa-ka-ree-ma-SEN* |
| Please speak slowly | *NO-ro-koo, ha-NAHSH-tay, koo-da-SA⌣ee* |

You have noticed by now that Japanese has a rhythm and tone of its own. This is very important in the language, and you should try to imitate the

8

phrases exactly as you hear them. For instance, compare the word for "yes," which you have just heard, with the word for "ash"

| | |
|---|---|
| Yes | *HA‿ee* |
| Ash | *ha‿EE* |

Now listen to the word for "no" followed by the word for "house."

| | |
|---|---|
| No | *EE‿yay* |
| House | *ee‿YAY* |

## LOCATION

When you need directions to get somewhere, you first name the place, add *wa*, and then add the expression for "where is?"

| | |
|---|---|
| Where is | *DO-ko dess-ka* |
| restaurant | *RESS-to-rahn* |
| Where is the restaurant? | *RESS-to-rahn-wa, DO-ko dess-ka?* |
| hotel | *HO-tay-roo* |
| | *or ya-do-ya* |
| Where is the hotel? | *HO-tay-roo-wa, DO-ko dess-ka?* |
| | *or ya-do-ya-wa, DO-ko dess-ka?* |
| station | *TAY‿ee-sha-ba* |

Hokkaido

10

| English | Japanese |
|---|---|
| **Where is the station?** | *TA Y ee-sha-ba-wa, DO-ko dess-ka?* |
| **toilet** | *BEN-jo* |
| **Where is the toilet?** | *BEN-jo-wa, DO-ko dess-ka?* |

## DIRECTION

The answer to your question "Where is such and such?" may be "To the right" or "To the left" or "Straight ahead," so you need to know these phrases.

**It's to the right** *MEENG-ee DESS*

**It's to the left** *hee-DA-ree DESS*

**It's straight ahead** *maht-TSOONG-oo SA-kee DESS*

It is sometimes useful to say "Please guide me there."

**Please guide me there** *ahn-NA ee-shtay koo-da-SA ee*

## NUMBERS

You need to know the numbers.

| | | | |
|---|---|---|---|
| **One** | *ee-CHEE* | **Three** | *SAHN* |
| **Two** | *NEE* | **Four** | *SHEE* |

| English | Japanese | | |
|---------|----------|---------|----------|
| Five | GO | Eight | ha-CHEE |
| Six | ro-KOO | Nine | KOO |
| Seven | shee-CHEE | Ten | JOO‿oo |

For "eleven," "twelve," and so on, you say "ten one," "ten two," and so on.

| Eleven | JOO‿oo ee-CHEE |
|--------|----------------|
| Twelve | JOO‿oo NEE |

For "twenty," "thirty," and so on, you say "two ten," "three ten," "four ten," and so on.

| Twenty | NEE-joo‿oo |
|--------|------------|
| Thirty | SAHN-joo‿oo |
| Forty | shee-JOO‿oo |

"Twenty-one," "thirty-two," and so on are formed exactly like English.

| Twenty-one | NEE-joo‿oo ee-CHEE |
|------------|--------------------|
| Twenty-two | NEE-joo‿oo NEE |
| One hundred | h‿ya-KOO |

Shinto Shrine

## WHAT'S THIS?

If you want to know the name of something, you can say "What's this?" and point to the thing you mean.

| English | Japanese |
|---|---|
| This | *ko-RAY* |
| what | *NA-nee* |
| | *or NAHN* |
| is it | *DESS-ka* |
| **What's this?** | *KO-ray-wa, NAHN-dess-ka?* |

Notice that there are certain small words like *wa* and *ka* that are put in to complete the expression. *wa* is added on to show the subject of a sentence; *ka* is always added on to a question. If you want something, you can use the phrase "Give me" and put the word you need before it, followed by the word *wo* which is used to show the object.

Imperial palace

Festival at the Heian Shrine, Kyoto

## ASKING FOR THINGS

| *English* | *Japanese* |
|---|---|
| **Give me** | *koo-da-SA⌣ee* |
| **cigarettes** | *ta-BA-ko* |
| **Give me cigarettes** | *ta-BA-ko-wo koo-da-SA⌣ee* |

*koo-da-SA⌣ee* is a polite expression, about like saying "Please grant." You find it in many expressions where it seems to mean "let," "permit," or "please."

| food | *ta-bay-MO-no* |
| Give me food | *ta-bay-MO-no-wo koo-da-SA⌣ee* |

Here are the words for some of the things you may require:

| bread | *PAHN* |
| cooked rice | *GO-hahn* |
| raw rice grains | *ko-MAY* |
| butter | *BA-ta* |
| eggs | *ta-MAHNG-o* |
| meat | *nee-KOO* |
| beef | *G⌣YOO⌣oo  nee-KOO* |
| pork | *boo-TA  nee-KOO* |
| chicken | *KAY⌣ee  nee-KOO* |
| fowl (in general) | *to-REE  nee-KOO* |
| potatoes | *ee-MO* |
| peas or beans | *ma-MAY* |

**16**

| English | Japanese |
|---------|----------|
| carrots | *neen-jeen* |
| onions | *NENG-ee* |
| cucumbers | *K⌣YOO⌣oo-ree* |
| apples | *reeng-c* |
| oranges | *o-REN-jee* |
| strawberries | *ee-cheeng-o* |
| fish | *sa-ka-na* |
| water | *mee-ZOO* |
| milk | *MEE-roo-koo* |
| sugar | *sa-TO⌣o* |
| salt | *shee⌣O* |
| matches | *MAHT-chee* |
| beer | *BEE⌣ee-roo* |
| coffee | *ko⌣o-HEE⌣ee* |
| Japanese dish of meat and vegetables | *skee-ya-kee* |
| soup | *swee-mo-NO* |

# HOW MUCH!

To find out how much things cost, you say:

| English | Japanese |
|---------|----------|
| How much | EE-koo-ra |
| is it | DESS-ka |

**How much is it?** *EE-koo-ra DESS-ka?*

# TIME

When you want to know the time, you say:

**What time is it?** *NAHN-jee DESS-ka?*

**It's two o'clock** *NEE-jee dess*

**It's three o'clock** *SAHN-jee dess*

**It's six o'clock** *ro-KOO-jee dess*

"Half past six" is "six o'clock, half."

**Half past six** *ro-KOO-jee HAHN*

"Ten past six" is "six o'clock, ten minutes past.

**Ten past six** *ro-KOO-jee joop_POON soong-ee*

**18**

"The Actor Onoe as a Samurai Going...", Utagawa Toyokuni

| _English_ | _Japanese_ |
| --- | --- |

"Twenty to seven" is said "seven o'clock, twenty minutes before."

| Twenty to seven | _shee-CHEE-jee nee-joop POON MA ay_ |
| --- | --- |

"Quarter of two" is "two o'clock, fifteen minutes before."

| Quarter of two | _NEE-jee JOO oo-go-FOON MA ay_ |
| --- | --- |

If you want to know when a movie starts or when a train leaves, you say:

| The train | _kee-SHA_ |
| --- | --- |
| when | _EET-soo_ |
| does it leave | _day-MA-ska_ |
| When does the train leave? | _kee-SHA-wa, EET-soo day-MA-ska?_ |
| The movie | _kaht-soo-DO o_ |
| when | _EET-soo_ |
| does it start | _ha-jee-ma-ree-MA-ska_ |
| When does the movie start? | _kaht-soo-DO o-wa EET-soo ha-jee-ma-ree-MA-ska?_ |
| Year | _to-SHEE_ _or_ NEN |
| month | _tsoo-KEE_ |

| English | Japanese |
|---------|----------|
| Week | *SHOO‿oo* |
| Day | *HEE* |
|  | *or nee-CHEE* |
| Yesterday | *kee-NO‿o* |
| Today | *K‿YO‿o* |
| Tomorrow | *ahsh-TA* |
| Day before yesterday | *eess-SA-koo-jeet-soo* |
| Day after tomorrow | *a-SAHT‿tay* |

The days of the week are:

| Sunday | *nee-chee-YO‿o-bee* |
|--------|---------------------|
| Monday | *get-soo-YO‿o-bee* |
| Tuesday | *ka-YO‿o-bee* |
| Wednesday | *soo‿ee-YO‿o-bee* |
| Thursday | *mo-koo-YO‿o-bee* |
| Friday | *keen-YO‿o-bee* |
| Saturday | *do-YO‿o-bee* |

The points of the compass are:

| North | *kee-TA* |
|-------|----------|
| East | *heeng-A-shee* |

| English | Japanese |
|---------|----------|
| South | mee-NA-mee |
| West | nee-SHEE |
| | |
| here | ko-KO |
| there | a-SKO |
| near | chee-KA ⌣ee |
| far | to ⌣o-EE ⌣ee |
| Is it far? | to ⌣o-EE ⌣ee dess-ka? |

## OTHER USEFUL PHRASES

The following phrases will be useful:

To find out someone's name you say, "Your name, what is it?"

| | |
|---|---|
| Your name | a-NA-ta-no na-MA ⌣ay |
| What is your name? | a-NA-ta-no na-MA ⌣ay-wa, NAHN dess-ka? |
| My name is John | wa-TAHK-shee-no na-WA JOHN dess |
| How do you say *pencil* in Japanese? | PENCIL wa, nee-HOHNG-go-day, NAHN-to ee ⌣ee-MA-ska? |
| Good night | go-keeng-en-YO ⌣o |
| Goodbye | sa-yo-NA-ra |

**22**

"Narumi", Ando Hiroshige

23

# ADDITIONAL EXPRESSIONS

| English | Japanese |
|---------|----------|
| I am an American | *wa-TAHK-shee-wa a-MAY-ree-ka-jeen DESS* |
| I am hungry | *ha-RA-ga HET_tay ee-MAHSS* |
| I am lost | *mee-CHEE-nee ma_ee-YOHT_ta* |
| I am sick | *wa-TAHK-shee-wa B_YO_o-kee dess* |
| I am thirsty | *NO-do-ga ka-WA_ee-tay ee-MAHSS* |
| I am wounded | *kay-GA-wo shtay-ee-MAHSS* |
| Stop! | *to-MA-ray!* |
| Come here! | *ko-KO-nee KO_ee!* |
| Quickly | *HA_ee-ya-koo* |
| Come quickly! | *HA_ee-ya-koo KO_ee!* |
| Go quickly! | *HA_ee-ya-koo ee-KAY!* |
| Help! | *ta-SKAY-tay koo-RAY!* |
| Bring help! | *ka-SAY_ee-wo ta-NO-moo!* |
| I will pay you | *KA-nay-wo ha-RAHT-tay YA-roo* |
| How far is the nearest village? | *ee-chee-BAHN chee-KA_ee MA-chee MA-day, DO-no koo-RA_ee-ka?* |

24

| English | Japanese |
|---|---|
| Is it far? | to‿o-EE-ka? |
| Is it near? | chee-KA‿ee-ka? |
| How far is it? | do-no koo-RA‿ee-ka? |
| Which way is north? | kee-TA-wa, do-chee-RA-ka? |
| Which is the road to___? | ___ay, YOO-koo mee-CHEE-wa, DO-ko dess-ka? |
| Draw me a map | CHEE-zoo-wo KA-kay |
| Take me there | so-KO-ay tsoo-RAY-tay yoo-KAY |
| Take me to a doctor | ee-SHA-ay tsoo-RAY-tay yoo-KAY |
| Take me to the hospital | B‿YO‿o-een-ay tsoo-RAY-tay yoo-KAY |
| Danger! | a-boo-NA‿ee! |
| Be careful! | CHOO-ee SAY‿ee-o! |
| Wait a minute! | MAHT‿tay koo-RAY! |

Banrukun rock gardens

# FILL-IN SENTENCES

In this section you will find a number of sentences, each containing a blank which can be filled in with any one of the words in the list that follows. For example, in order to say "I want some soap," look for the phrase "I want___" in the English column and find the Japanese expression given beside it; in this case it is ___ wo, koo-da-SA_ee. Then look for the word "soap" in the list that follows; the Japanese is sek-KEN. Put the word for "soap" in the blank space and you get sek-KEN-wo koo-da-SA_ee.

Notice that Japanese word-order is different from. English; thus, the Japanese for "I want soap" or "Give me soap" is really "Soap please give."

There are two other points in these sentences which you should notice. The first is that in Japanese you don't say "I have___" or "Do you have any___" but "___there is" or "___is there?" The second is that you don't need to use "I" or "you" or "he" in Japanese sentences like these or in most other places where these words are used in English.

| English | Japanese |
|---|---|
| **Please give me___** | ___wo, koo-da-SA_ee |
| **Bring me___** | ___wo, MOHT_tay kee-TAY koo-da-SA_ee |
| **Where can I get___?** | ___wa, DO-ko-nee a-ree-MA-ska? |

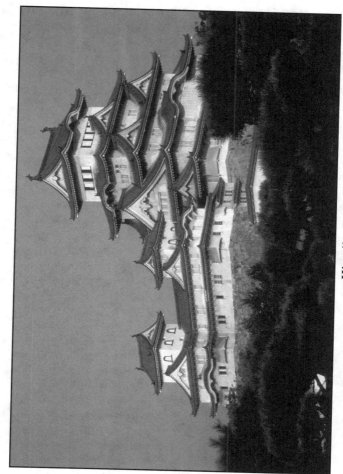

Himeji castle

**Shinto temple**

| English | Japanese |
|---------|----------|
| I have___ | ___wa, a-ree-MAHSS |
| I don't have___ | ___wa, a-ree-ma-SEN |
| Have you___? | ___wa, a-ree-MA-ska? |

## EXAMPLE

| Have you___? | ___wa, a-ree-MA-ska? |
|---------|----------|
| food | ta-bay-MO-no |

**Have you food?** ta-bay-MO-no-wa, a-ree-MA-ska?

| | |
|---------|----------|
| food | ta-bay-MO-no |
| meal | go-HAHN |
| wheat-rice mixture | moo-gee-GO-hahn |
| drinking water | no-mee-MEE-zoo |
| pickled plums | oo-MAY bo‿o-SHEE |
| pickled things to go with rice | tsoo-KAY-mo-no |
| pork stew | boo-TA JEE-roo |
| soy-bean soup | mee-so-SHEE-roo |

| English | Japanese |
|---|---|
| tea | o-CHA |
| white radishes | DA⁀ee-kohn |
| | |
| a cup | KOHP⁀poo |
| a fork | FO⁀o-koo |
| a knife | NA⁀ee-foo |
| a plate | sa-ra |
| a spoon | sa-jee |
| | |
| a bathroom | foo-ro-BA |
| a bed | sheen-DA⁀ee |
| bedding | foo-TOHN |
| a blanket | MO⁀o-foo |
| a mosquito net | ka-YA |
| a room | hay-YA |
| a sleeping mat (Japanese style) | nay-do-KO |
| cigars | ha-MA-kee |
| a pipe | PA⁀ee-poo |
| tobacco or cigarettes | ta-BA-ko |
| ink | EEN-koo |

| English | Japanese |
|---|---|
| a pen | PEN |
| a pencil | en-PEET-soo |
| a comb | koo-SHEE |
| hot water | o-YOO |
| a razor | ka-mee-SO-ree |
| razor blades | ka-mee-SO-ree-no HA |
| soap | sek-KEN |
| a toothbrush | ha-MEE-ga-kee YO‿o-jee |
| tooth powder | ha-mee-GA-kee KO |
| a handkerchief | HAHN-ka-chee |
| a raincoat | RAY‿een-ko‿o-to |
| a shirt | SHAHT-soo |
| shoe laces | KOOT-soo hee-MO |
| shoe polish | koot-soo MEE-ga-kee |
| shoes | KOOT-soo |
| a towel | TAY-no-goo‿ee |
| underwear | shta-GEE |
| buttons | bo-TAHN |
| a needle | HA-ree |

| English | Japanese |
|---|---|
| safety pins | *ahn-zen-PEEN* |
| thread | *EE-to* |
| | |
| aspirin | *a-soo-PEE-reen* |
| a bandage | *ho‿o-TA‿ee* |
| cotton | *wa-TA* |
| a disinfectant | *SHO‿o-do-koo ZA‿ee* |
| a laxative | *TSOO‿oo-jee GOO-soo-ree* |
| sun glasses | *ee-RO MAY-ga-nay* |
| I want to___ | *wa-TAHK-shee-wa___ TA‿ee* |

**EXAMPLE**

| | |
|---|---|
| I want to___ | *wa-TAHK-shee-wa___ TA‿ee* |
| rest | *ya-soo-mee* |
| I want to rest | *wa-TAHK-shee-wa ya-soo-mee-TA‿ee* |
| sleep | *nay* |
| wash up | *a-ra‿ee* |
| bathe | *o-YOO-nee, ha‿ee-ree* |
| go to the barber | *to-ko-YA-ay yoo-kee* |
| be shaved | *hee-gay wa-so-ree* |
| buy___ | *___wa ka‿ee-TA‿ee* |

30

Kiyomizu Temple, Kyoto

**Statue of Buddha**

| English | Japanese |
|---------|----------|
| _Where is a___?_ | |
| _Where are___?_ | ___wa, DO-ko dess-ka? |
| _Where is the___?_ | |

**EXAMPLE**

| Where is___ | ___wa, DO-ko dess-ka |
|-------------|----------------------|
| the main street | hohn-DO‿o-ree |
| Where is the main street? | hohn-DO‿o-ree-wa, DO-ko dess-ka? |

| | |
|--|--|
| a barber | to-ko-YA |
| a dentist | HA‿ee-sha |
| a doctor | ee-SHA |
| a laborer | neen-POO |
| a mechanic | nay-KA-neek |
| a policeman | JOON-sa |
| a servant | |
|   man | GAY-nahn |
|   woman | jo-CHOO |
| a shoemaker | koot-SOO-ya |
| a tailor | yo‿o-foo-koo-YA |
| a bridge | ha-SHEE |

| English | Japanese |
|---|---|
| a bus | *BA-soo* |
| a church | *k͜yo͜o-KA͜ee* |
| the city | *shee* |
| a drugstore | *koo-soo-ree-YA* |
| a footpath *or* trail | *ko-mee-chee* |
| a garage | *ga-RAY͜ee-jee* |
| a hospital | *B͜YO͜o-een* |
| a laundry | *sen-TA-koo-ya* |
| the main street | *hohn-DO͜o-ree* |
| the market place | *ee-chee-BA* |
| the ocean | *OO-mee* |
| the police station | *kay͜ee-SAHT-soo-SHO* |
| the post-office and telegraph office | *yoo͜oo-BEENK-yo-koo* |
| the river | *ka-WA* |
| the road | *mee-CHEE* |
| a spring | *ee-zoo-MEE* |
| a store | *mee-SAY* |

| English | Japanese |
|---------|----------|
| a telephone | *DEN-wa* |
| the town | *ma-CHEE* |
| the village | *moo-RA* |
| a well | *EE-do* |

---

It is___          ___*dess*

**EXAMPLE**

| English | Japanese |
|---------|----------|
| It is___ | ___*dess* |
| near | *chee-KA ͜ee* |
| It is near | *chee-KA ͜ee dess* |
| far | *to ͜o-EE* |
| near | *chee-KA ͜ee* |
| hot | *aht-SOO ͜ee* |
| cold | *sa-MOO ͜ee* |
| good | *yo-ro-SHEE* |
| bad | *wa-ROO ͜ee* |
| expensive | *ta-KA ͜ee* |
| too expensive | *ta-ka-soo-GEE-roo* |

**33**

# IMPORTANT SIGNS

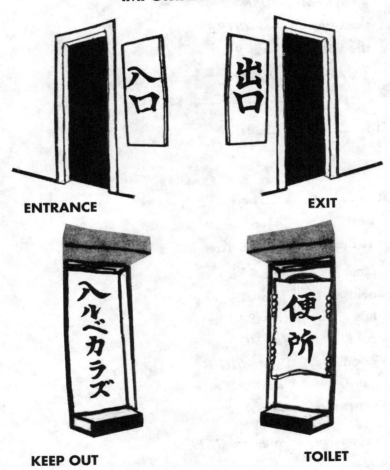

**ENTRANCE**

**EXIT**

**KEEP OUT**

**TOILET**

**STOP**

**BE CAREFUL**

**HIGH TENSION WIRES**

**DANGER**

# ALPHABETICAL WORD LIST

## A

| *English* | *Japanese* |
|---|---|
| American | *a-may-ree-KA-no* |
| I am an American | *wa-TAHK-shee-wa a-MAY-ree-ka-jeen DESS* |
| apples | *reeng-o* |
| aspirin | *a-soo-PEE-reen* |

## B

| | |
|---|---|
| bad | *wa-ROO⌣ee –* |
| bandage | *ho⌣o-TA⌣ee* |

Guardian statue

| English | Japanese |
|---------|----------|
| barber | *to-ko-YA* |
| bathroom | *foo-ro-BA* |
| be shaved | |
| **I want to be** shaved | *wa-TAHK-shee-wa hee-gay-wo so-ree-TA ⌣ee* |
| beans | *ma-MAY* |
| Be careful! | *CHOO⌣ee SAY⌣ee-o!* |
| bed | *sheen-DA ⌣ee* |
| bedding | *foo-TOHN* |
| beef | *G⌣YOO⌣oo-nee-koo* |
| beer | *BEE⌣ee-roo* |
| blanket | *MO⌣o-foo* |
| bread | *PAHN* |
| bridge | *ha-SHEE* |
| bring | |
| **Bring help!** | *ka-SAY⌣ee-wo ta-NO-moo!* |
| **Bring me___** | *___wo MOHT⌣tay KEE-tay koo-da-SA ⌣ee* |
| bus | *BA-soo* |
| butter | *BA-ta* |

| English | Japanese |
|---------|----------|
| buttons | *bo-TAHN* |
| buy | |
|   I want to buy___ | *___wo ka⌣ee-TA⌣ee* |

## C

| | |
|---------|----------|
| careful | |
|   Be careful! | *CHOO⌣ee SAY⌣ee-o!* |
| carrots | *neen-jeen* |
| chicken | *KAY⌣ee-nee-koo* |
| church | *k⌣yo⌣o-KA⌣ee* |
| cigarettes | *ta-BA-ko* |
| cigars | *ha-MA-kee* |
| city | *shee* |
| coffee | *ko⌣o-HEE⌣ee* |
| comb | *koo꞊SHEE* |
| Come! | *KO⌣ee!* |
|   Come here! | *ko-KO-nee KO⌣ee!* |
|   Come quickly! | *HA⌣ee-ya-koo KO⌣ee!* |
| cooked rice | *GO-hahn* |

| English | Japanese |
|---------|----------|
| cotton | wa-TA |
| cover | |
|   Take cover! | KA-gay-nee HA ⏝ee-rayl |
| cucumbers | K ⏝ YOO ⏝oo-ree |
| cup | KOHP ⏝poo |

## D

| | |
|---|---|
| Danger! | a-boo-NA ⏝ee! |
| day | HEE |
|   day after tomorrow | a-SAHT ⏝tay |
|   day before yesterday | eess-SA-koo-jeet-soo |
|   Good day | KOHN nee-chee-WA |
| dentist | HA ⏝ee-sha |
| disinfectant | SHO ⏝o-do-koo ZA ⏝ee |
| Do you understand? | wa-ka-ree-MA-sta-ka? |
| doctor | ee-SHA |
|   Take me to a doctor | ee-SHA-ay soo-RAY-tay yoo-KAY |

| English | Japanese |
|---------|----------|
| drinking water | *no-mee-MEE-soo* |
| a drugstore | *koo-soo-ree-YA* |

## E

| | |
|---|---|
| east | *heeng-A-shee* |
| eggs | *ta-MAHNG-o* |
| eight | *ha-CHEE* |
| eleven | *JOO⌣oo ee-CHEE* |
| evening | |
| Good evening | *kohn-BAHN-wa* |
| expensive | *ta-KA⌣ee* |
| too expensive | *ta-ka-soo-GEE-roo* |

## F

| | |
|---|---|
| far | *to⌣o-EE⌣ee* |
| How far is it? | *do-no koo-RA⌣ee-ka?* |
| fish | *sa-ka-na* |
| five | *GO* |
| food | *ta-bay-MO-no* |

Rock garden

Local restaurant

| English | Japanese |
|---------|----------|
| footpath | *ko-mee-CHEE* |
| fork | *FO⌣o-koo* |
| forty | *shee-JOO⌣oo* |
| four | *SHEE* |
| Friday | *KEEN YO⌣o-bee* |

## G

| | |
|---------|----------|
| garage | *ga-RAY⌣ee-jee* |
| gas | *ga-so-REEN* |
| give | |
| Please give me___ | ___*wo, koo-da-SA⌣ee* |
| go | |
| Go quickly! | *HA⌣ee-ya-koo ee-KAY!* |
| good | *yo-ro-SHEE* |
| Good-by | *sa-yo-NA-ra* |
| Good day | *KOHN nee-chee-WA* |
| Good evening | *kohn-BAHN-wa* |

| English | Japanese |
|---|---|
| guide | |
| Please guide me there | *ahn-NA⌣ee-shtay koo-da-SA⌣ee* |

## H

| half | *HAHN* |
|---|---|
| half past six | *ro-KOO-jee HAHN* |
| handkerchief | *HAHN-ka-chee* |
| have | |
| Have you___? | *___wa, a-ree-MA-ska?* |
| I have___ | *___wa, a-ree-MAHSS* |
| I don't have___ | *___wa, a-ree-ma-SEN* |
| he | *KA-ray* |
| Help! | *ta-SKAY-tay koo-RAY!* |
| Bring help! | *ka-SAY⌣ee-wo ta-NO-moo* |
| here | *ko-KO* |
| Come here! | *ko-KO-nee KO⌣o⌣ee!* |
| hospital | *B⌣YO⌣o-een* |

| English | Japanese |
|---|---|
| Take me to the hospital | B‿YO‿o-een-ay tsoo-RAY-tay yoo-KAY |
| hot | aht-SOO‿ee |
| hot water | o-YOO |
| hotel | HO-tay-roo *or* ya-do-ya |
| Where is the hotel? | HO-tay-roo-wa, DO-ko dess-ka? *or* ya-do-ya-wa, DO-ko dess-ka? |
| house | ee‿YAY |
| how | |
| How much? | EE-koo-ra? |
| How do you say__in Japanese? | ___wa, nee-HOHN-go day, NAHN-to ee‿ee-MA-ska? |
| hundred | h‿ya-KOO |
| hungry | |
| I am hungry | ha-RA-ga HET‿tay ee-MAHSS |

# I

|  |  |
|---|---|
|  | wa-TAHK-shee |
| ink | EEN-koo |

| English | Japanese |
|---------|----------|
| **is** | |
| Is it? | *DESS-ka?* |
| What is it? | *NAHN dess-ka?* |
| Where is it? | *DO-ko dess-ka?* |

## J

| | |
|---|---|
| Japanese | *nee-HOHN-go* |
| in Japanese | *nee-HOHN-go-day* |
| Japanese dish of meat and vegetables | *skee-ya-kee* |

## K

| | |
|---|---|
| knife | *NA⌣ee-foo* |

## L

| | |
|---|---|
| laborer | *neen-POO* |
| laundry | *sen-TA-koo-ya* |
| a laxative | *TSOO⌣oo-jee GOO-soo-ree* |
| **leave** | |
| When does the train leave? | *kee-SHA-wa EET-soo day-MA-ska?* |

| English | Japanese |
|---------|----------|
| left | |
| It's to the left | *hee-DA-ree DESS* |
| lost | |
| I am lost | *mee-CHEE-nee ma⌣ee-YOHT⌣ta* |

## M

| | |
|---------|----------|
| the main street | *hohn-DO⌣o-ree* |
| a map | *CHEE-zoo* |
| Draw me a map | *CHEE-zoo-wo KA-kay* |
| the market place | *ee-chee-BA* |
| matches | *MAHT-chee* |
| a meal | *go-HAHN* |
| meat | *nee-KOO* |
| a mechanic | *may-KA-neek* |
| milk | *MEE-roo-koo* |
| Monday | *get-soo-YO⌣o-bee* |
| month | *tsoo-KEE* |
| mosquito net | *ka-YA* |

| English | Japanese |
|---|---|
| the movie | kaht-soo-DO‿o |
| What time does the movie start? | kaht-soo-DO‿o-wa, EET-soo ha-jee-ma·ree-MA-ska? |

## N

| | |
|---|---|
| name | na-MA‿ay |
| My name is___ | wa-TAHK-shee-no na-WA__dess |
| What's your name? | a-NA-ta-no na-MA‿ay-wa, NAHN dess-ka? |
| near | chee-KA‿ee |
| nearest | ee-chee-BAHN chee-KA‿ee |
| the nearest town | ee-chee-BAHN chee-KA‿ee ma-CHEE |
| needle | HA-ree |
| nine | KOO |
| no | EE‿yay |
| north | kee-TA |
| Which way is north? | kee-TA-wa, do-chee-RA-ka? |

Buddha

Japanese block print

| English | Japanese |
|---------|----------|

## O

**of**

    quarter of two     *NEE-jee JOO‿oo-go-FOON ma‿yay*

**one**     *ee-CHEE*

**one hundred**     *h‿ya-KOO*

**oranges**     *o-REN-jee*

## P

**pardon me**     *sheet-SOO-ray‿ee*

    Pardon me a moment     *CHOH1‿to, sheet-SOO-ray‿ee*

**peas**     *ma-MAY*

**pen**     *PEN*

**pencil**     *en-PEET-soo*

**pickled plums**     *oo-MAY bo‿o-SHEE*

**pickled things to eat with rice**     *tsoo-KAY-mo-no*

**pins**

    safety pins     *ahn-zen-PEEN*

| English | Japanese |
|---------|----------|
| a pipe | *PA ⁀ee-poo* |
| plate | *sa-ra* |
| Please | *koo-da-SA ⁀ee* |
| Please guide me there | *ahn-NA ⁀ee-shtay koo-da-SA ⁀ee* |
| Please speak slowly | *NO-ro-koo, ha-NAHSH-tay koo-da-SA ⁀ee* |
| policeman | *JOON-sa* |
| the police station | *kay ⁀ee-SAHT-soo SHO* |
| pork | *boo-TA nee-KOO* |
| pork stew | *boo-TA JEE-roo* |
| post office and telegraph office | *yoo ⁀oo-BEENK-yo-koo* |
| potatoes | *ee-MO* |

## Q

| | |
|---------|----------|
| Quickly! | *HA ⁀ee-ya-koo!* |
| Come quickly! | *HA ⁀ee-ya-koo KO ⁀o ⁀ee!* |
| Go quickly! | *HA ⁀ee-ya-koo ee-KAY! ·* |

| English | Japanese |
|---------|----------|

## R

| | |
|---------|----------|
| raincoat | *RAY⌣een-ko⌣oto* |
| razor | *ka-mee-SO-ree* |
|   razor blades | *ka-mee-SO-ree-no HA* |
| rest | |
|   I want to rest | *wa-TAHK-shee-wa ya-soo-mee-TA⌣ee* |
| a restaurant | *RESS-to-rahn* |
|   Where is a restaurant? | *RESS-to-rahn-wa, DO-ko dess-ka?* |
| rice | |
|   cooked rice | *GO-hahn* |
|   raw rice grains | *ko-MAY* |
| right | |
|   It's to the right | *MEENG-ee DESS* |
| river | *ka-WA* |
| road | *mee-CHEE* |
| a room | *hay-YA* |

| English | Japanese |
|---------|----------|

## S

| safety pins | *ahn-zen-PEEN* |
|-------------|----------------|
| sailors | *SWEE-hay* |
| salt | *shee-O* |
| Saturday | *do-YO⌣o-bee* |
| say | |

How do you say____in Japanese?  *____wa, nee-HOHN-go-day, NAHN-to ee⌣ee-MA-ska?*

| servant | |
|---------|---|
| man | *GAY-nahn* |
| woman | *jo-CHOO* |
| seven | *shee-CHEE* |
| shave | |

I want to be shaved  *hee-gay-wo so-ree-TA⌣ee*

Incense burning ritual

Wish tree-heian, Jingu shrine

| English | Japanese |
|---|---|
| she | *KA-no-jo* |
| shirt | *SHAHT-soo* |
| shoes | *KOOT-soo* |
| shoe laces | *KOOT-soo hee-MO* |
| shoemaker | *koot-SOO-ya* |
| shoe polish | *KOOT-soo MEE-ga-kee* |
| sick | *B⌣YO⌣o-kee* |
| six | *ro-KOO* |
| sleep | |
| I want to sleep | *wa-TAHK-shee-wa nay-TA⌣ee* |
| sleeping mat (Japanese style) | *nay-do-KO* |
| slowly | *NO-ro-koo* |
| soap | *sek-KEN* |
| south | *mee-NA-mee* |
| soy-bean soup | *mee-so-SHEE-roo* |
| speak | |
| Please speak slowly | *NO-ro-koo, ha-NAHSH-tay koo-da-SA⌣ee* |

| English | Japanese |
|---------|----------|
| a spring | *ee-zoo-MEE* |
| start | |
| When does the movie start? | *kaht-soo-DO◡o-wa, EET-soo ha-jee-ma-ree-MA-ska?* |
| station | |
| railroad station | *TAY◡ee-sha-ba* |
| police station | *kay◡ee-SAHT-soo SHO◡o* |
| Where is the station? | *TAY◡ee-sha-ba-wa, DO-ko dess-ka?* |
| Stop! | *to-MA-ray!* |
| store | *mee-SAY* |
| strawberries | *ee-cheeng-o* |
| straight ahead | |
| It's straight ahead | *maht-SOONG-oo SA-kee DESS* |
| street | |
| the main street | *hohn-DO◡o-ree* |
| sugar | *sa-TO◡o* |
| Sunday | *nee-chee-YO◡o-bee* |

52

| *English* | *Japanese* |
|---|---|
| tailor | *yo‿o-foo-koo-YA* |
| **take** | |
|   Take cover! | *KA-gay-nee HA‿ee-ray!* |
|   Take me there | *so-KO-ay tsoo-RAY-tay yoo-KAY* |
|   Take me to a doctor | *ee-SHA-ay tsoo-RAY-tay yoo-KAY* |
|   Take me to the hospital | *B‿YO‿o-een-ay tsoo-RAY-tay yoo-KAY* |
| tea | *o-CHA* |
| telegraph office | *yoo‿oo-BEENK-yo-koo* |
| telephone | *DEN-wa* |
| ten | *JOO‿oo* |
|   ten minutes past six | *ro-KOO-jee joop‿POON soong-ee* |
| Thank you | *a-REENG-a-to‿o* |
| there | *a-SKO* |
|   Take me there | *so-KO-ay tsoo-RAY-tay yoo-KAY* |
| they | *KA-ray-ra* |

| English | Japanese |
|---|---|
| They are___ thirsty | *KA-ray-ra-wa___dess* |
| I am thirsty | *NO-do-ga ka-WA⌣ee-tay ee-MAHSS* |
| this | *ko-RAY* |
| What's this? | *KO-ray-wa, NAHN dess-ka?* |
| thread | *EE-to* |
| three | *SAHN* |
| It's three o'clock | *SAHN-jee dess* |
| Thursday | *mo-koo-YO⌣o-bee* |
| time | |
| What time is it? | *NAHN-jee DESS-ka?* |
| to | |
| to a doctor | *ee-SHA-ay* |
| to a hospital | *B⌣YO⌣o-een-ay* |
| to the left | *hee-DA-ree* |
| to the right | *MEENG-ee* |
| twenty to seven | *shee-CHEE-jee nee-joop⌣POON MA⌣ay* |
| tobacco | *ta-BA-ko* |

54

Rice planting

**Tokyo tower**

| English | Japanese |
|---------|----------|
| today | K‿YO‿o |
| toilet | BEN-jo |
| Where is the toilet? | BEN-jo-wa, DO-ko dess-ka? |
| tomorrow | ahsh-TA |
| day after tomorrow | a-SAHT‿tay |
| too | |
| too expensive | ta-ka-soo-GEE-roo |
| toothbrush | ha-MEE-ga-kee YO‿o-jee |
| tooth powder | ha-mee-GA-kee KO |
| towel | TAY-no-goo‿ee |
| town | ma-CHEE |
| the nearest town | ee-chee-BAHN chee-KA‿ee ma-CHEE |
| trail *or* footpath | ko-mee-CHEE |
| train | kee-SHA |
| What time does the train leave? | kee-SHA-wa, EET-soo day-MA-ska? |
| Tuesday | ka-YO‿o-bee |

| English | Japanese |
|---------|----------|
| twelve | *JOO‿oo NEE* |
| twenty | *NEE-joo‿oo* |
| twenty-one | *NEE-joo‿oo ee-CHEE* |
| twenty-two | *NEE-joo‿oo NEE* |
| two | *NEE* |
| It's two o'clock | *NEE-jee dess* |
| quarter of two | *NEE-jee JOO‿oo-go-FOON ma‿ay* |

## U

| | |
|---|---|
| understand | |
| Do you understand | *wa-ka-ree-MA-SKA?* |
| I don't understand | *wa-ka-ree-ma-SEN* |
| underwear | *shta-GEE* |

## V

| | |
|---|---|
| village | *moo-RA* |

| English | Japanese |
|---------|----------|
| How far is the nearest village? | *ee-chee-BAHN chee-KA͡ee MA-chee MA-day, DO-no koo-RA͡ee-ka?* |

## W

**wait**

| | |
|---|---|
| Wait a minute! | *MAHT͡tay koo-RAY!* |

**want**

| | |
|---|---|
| I want to___ | *wa-TAHK-shee-wa___TA͡ee* |

**wash up**

| | |
|---|---|
| I want to wash up | *wa-TAHK-shee-wa a-ra͡ee-TA͡ee* |

| | |
|---|---|
| water | *MEE-zoo* |
| drinking water | *no-mee-MEE-zoo* |
| hot water | *o-YOO* |
| Wednesday | *SOO͡ee YO͡o-bee* |
| well (for water) | *EE-do* |
| west | *nee-SHEE* |
| what | *NA-nee* *or NAHN* |

| English | Japanese |
|---|---|
| What's this? | *KO-ray-wa, NAHN-dess-ka?* |
| What time is it? | *NAHN-jee DESS-ka?* |
| What's your name? | *a-NA-ta-no na-MA⌣ay-wa, NAHN dess-ka?* |
| when | *EET-soo* |
| When does the movie start? | *kaht-soo-DO⌣o-wa EET-soo ha-jee-ma-ree-MA-ska?* |
| When does the train leave? | *kee-SHA-wa, EET-soo day-MA-ska?* |
| where | *DO-ko* |
| Where is it? | *DO-ko dess-ka?* |
| Where are the American sailors? | *a-may-ree-KA-no SWEE-hay-wa, DO-ko dess-ka?* |
| Where are the sailors? | *SWEE-hay-wa, DO-ko dess-ka?* |
| Where can I get___? | *___wa, do-KO-nee a-ree-MA-ska?* |
| which | |
| Which is the road to___ | *___ay, YOO-koo mee-CHEE-wa, DO-ko dess-ka?* |

58

| English | Japanese |
|---|---|
| Which way is north? | kee-TA-wa, do-chee-RA-ka? |
| white radishes | DA‿ee-kohn |
| wounded | |
| I am wounded | kay-GA-wo shtay-ee-MAHSS |

## Y

| | | |
|---|---|---|
| year | | to-SHEE |
| | or | NEN |
| yes | | HA‿ee |
| yesterday | | kee-NO‿o |
| day before yesterday | | eess-SA-koo-jeet-soo |
| you | | |
| Do you understand? | | wa-ka-ree-MA-SKA? |
| Have you___? | | ___wa, a-ree-MA-ska? |
| I will pay you | | KA-nay-wo ha-RA-tay YA-roo |
| your name | | a-NA-ta-no na-MA‿ay |

**Peace memorial park**

Thanksgiving celebration

**Playing the five-string biwa**